ENCOURAGING WORDS FOR *Quiet Moments*

E5087

warnerpress

3058002100000324

Warner Press, Inc.

Warner Press and Warner Press logo are trademarks of Warner Press. Inc.

Editor: Julie Campbell

Cover and Layout by Katie Miller

Sometimes the most precious moments
in our lives happen when we least expect them.
And it's then we realize, though God's working
may sometimes seem invisible—it's not.

LINDA E. KNIGHT

We live by faith, not by sight.

2 CORINTHIANS 5:7 (NIV)

Have you ever gathered shells at the beach? Although you may find two that look alike, upon closer inspection you will find that there is always something different. This is also true about us. Although people may sometimes appear similar in their outward appearance, their talents, or personalities, we, too, are unique. God's design for our lives also differs for each individual. In Romans 12:6 (NIV), Paul teaches us that, *We have different gifts, according to the grace given to each of us.* Celebrate your God-given talent today, and by doing so, you will reflect your Creator's handiwork.

Is the uphill climb
getting to you?
Slow down a little—
let God set the rhythm
for your life.
Relax in God's arms;
let Him handle your day!

My grace is sufficient for you,
for my power is made perfect in weakness.

2 Corinthians 12:9 (NIV)

Most people would like to live in a world of peace and tranquility. A place where the storms of life wouldn't "rock their boat." We may look for that harbor of refuge by avoiding risky ventures or by never leaving our comfort zone. But God calls us from the pier and asks us to *launch out into the deep* (Luke 5:4). He promises us that in the midst of the storm, He is our safe harbor. So get into your boat and do what God has called you to do. Because no matter what storms we encounter, by anchoring ourselves to Him, we can be assured that He will calm the waves and return peace to our lives.

Nancy Otto Boffo

What a blessing it is to know
that God sees each success we celebrate,
each tear we cry, and each time
we give thanks to Him.
He sees it all—the hard,
the good, and the messy—
and He walks beside us always.

Julie Campbell

*God has said, "Never will I leave you;
never will I forsake you."*

Hebrews 13:5 (NIV)

Have you ever wondered what tomorrow might bring? At one time or another we've all thought about what may lie ahead. Sometimes the road we travel may appear to be crooked and confusing, but when our path seems to wind in directions that don't make sense, it is reassuring to know that God *is* in control. The Bible tells us that our life has been mapped out. When we trust in God, we can be assured that although there may be twists and turns along the way, with Him hope always waits around the corner.

Nancy Otto Boffo

Waiting may seem like wasted moments
when time stands still for you,
but God is working on your behalf,
watching over all you do.
He sees, He hears, He knows, and He cares.

REBECCA BARLOW JORDAN

Wait for the LORD*;*
be strong and take heart.

PSALM 27:14 (NIV)

When we reach the end of our strength, God enfolds us in His arms and warms us with His love. When the only place we can look is up, He is faithful to meet us and greet us at our point of need. God is with you, strengthening you and meeting your every need with His faithful arms of love.

Rebecca Barlow Jordan

It is God who arms me with strength.

Psalm 18:32 (NIV)

Be still and know…
that God is in control and knows the plan.
Be still and know…
that God knows your anxieties.
Be still and know…
that God has your back.
Be still and know…
that God sings over you and delights in you!

Leah Adams

Be still, and know that I am God.

Psalm 46:10 (niv)

Waiting teaches us patience. As we wait on the Lord, we learn life-lessons about what it really means to trust. Our faith is tested and proven strong and sure. We discover that Jesus is the true source of our hope and peace. And when Jesus is all that we have, we realize that Jesus is all that we need.

Robin Loisch

We wait in hope for the Lord;
he is our help and our shield.

Psalm 33:20 (NIV)

Hope is daring to imagine
that life is the way
you envision it to be,
and faith makes
that hope a reality.

CHERYL SMITH

"For I know the plans I have for you,"
declares the LORD, *"plans to prosper you*
and not to harm you,
plans to give you hope and a future."

JEREMIAH 29:11 (NIV)

Do you ever feel like God is a million miles away? Like you just don't feel His presence the way you should—or the way you think you should? If you've had this feeling before, I have good news for you: You have an all-access pass to God, the King of Kings, Creator of the Universe! Ephesians 2:17–18 (NIV) says: *He came and preached peace to you who were far away and peace to those who were near. For through him we both have access to the Father by one Spirit.* The God of the Universe has personally invited *you* to His backstage, off limits, members-only area. You have an all-access pass! No limits, no restrictions! What will you do with your access?

Julie Campbell

In times of confusion,
unfulfilled dreams,
heaviness of heart—
what a comfort to know
that our Heavenly Father
eagerly waits with open arms
to draw us into His embrace.
Hear His heartbeat
as He holds you close!

Karen Rhodes

Almost everyone has felt ignored in a crowd at one time or another. While this may be true in our earthly endeavors, it is never true of our standing with God. We can all pray with King David, *Keep me as the apple of your eye* (Psalm 17:8 NIV). That endearment describes how each of us appears to God. From Hebrew origins, the word *apple* used in the verse means *pupil*, and signifies our value and proximity to God. Our image remains fixed in His mind. His eye never strays. And He never, ever compares us to another. No matter where we go or what we do, He won't turn away from us—a fact that offers each of us unparalleled security. Among earth's billions, each face stands out to God.

I place no hope in my strength,
nor in my works:
but all my confidence
is in God my protector,
who never abandons those
who have put all their hope
and thought in him.

FRANCOIS RABELAIS

You have been my hope, Sovereign LORD,
my confidence since my youth.

PSALM 71:5 (NIV)

The Lord of the universe molded clay into mountains and water droplets into raging seas. He breathed life into Rocky Mountain wildflowers and placed beauty in ornate ocean coral. He commanded the colors of the sunrise to burst into view and the song of the winds to sweep over the plains. The Creator gently formed grains of sand in the deserts, knowing the very number that drifted into rolling hills and deep valleys. He, who knows the details of the sand in every desert, knows the details of your days as well. *The very hairs of your head are all numbered* (Matthew 10:30 NIV).

LAURA R. PITTMAN

In every quiet moment,
through every whispered prayer,
God speaks love to our hearts,
gently reminding us we're never alone.

JULIE CAMPBELL

*Do not be afraid; do not be discouraged,
for the* LORD *your God will be with you
wherever you go.*

JOSHUA 1:9 (NIV)

What anxieties or worries occupy your time? Do you worry about getting projects completed on time? Are you concerned about the organization of your home? At times do you become anxious as you add up the bills, hoping that one more recalculation would somehow cause the amount to diminish? In all your anxieties, remember that you are not without a comforter. Our Father tells us to *cast all (our) anxiety on him because he cares* (1 Peter 5:7 NIV). Give God your worries today.

Laura R. Pittman

Heart to heart,
God knows everything about us…
Every thought, every sigh,
every doubt, every fear,
every smile, every tear,
every longing…every reason
to open our hearts to Him.

LINDA E. KNIGHT

*But to all who believed him and accepted him,
he gave the right to become children of God.*

JOHN 1:12 (NLT)

It's amazing to look up through the branches of a tall tree. A pine or redwood seems to rise to the heavens. Who would ever have thought that such a tall and mighty tree could grow from a tiny seed? God can also take the small and simple things in our lives and transform them into towering successes. In Ephesians 3:20–21 (NIV) we read, *Now to him who is able to do immeasurably more than all we ask or imagine, according to his power that is at work within us, to him be glory.* This Scripture reminds us that God is not limited by the size of our ideas. No matter how big or small our hopes or dreams, let's remember that *with God all things are possible* (Matthew 19:26 NIV).

Be on the lookout for mercies.
The more we look for them,
the more of them we will see…
Better to lose count
while naming your blessings
than to lose your blessings
to counting your troubles.

MALTBIE D. BABCOCK

O LORD my God, you have performed many wonders for us…. If I tried to recite all your wonderful deeds, I would never come to the end of them.

PSALM 40:5 (NLT)

The shimmering sheets of color that engulf a sunrise swell across the shoreline, melting into waves of foam. The beauty of the moment lingers, painting minutes into memories. In time the colors fade and the sky becomes a sea of blues and grays, sweeping away the mist of the morning. As quickly as the fading of the sunrise and the loss of the morning mist, the Lord of the universe sweeps away our sins. *I have swept away your offenses like a cloud, your sins like the morning mist. Return to me, for I have redeemed you* (Isaiah 44:22 NIV).

Peace is not the absence of conflict,
but the presence of God
no matter what the conflict.

I am leaving you with a gift—
peace of mind and heart.
And the peace I give
is a gift the world cannot give.
So don't be troubled or afraid.

John 14:27 (NLT)

Some of us enjoy solitude more than others. Whether we revel in time alone or long for companionship, there is one journey that we must make all by ourselves—our walk of faith. We cannot hold another responsible for the decisions we make on that trip; our choices are ours alone. But even in our personal solitude, we have a Friend. God has marvelously provided for us by sending His Spirit to indwell us, allowing us to carry within the Person who will never forsake us. *Fear thou not; for I am with thee...I will strengthen thee; yea, I will help thee*, God promises in Isaiah 41:10. In those times when the road of faith seems hard and lonely, remember God is beside and within you, guiding you safely to His perfect will.

Listen, my friend! Your helplessness is your best prayer. It calls from your heart to the heart of God with greater effect than all your uttered pleas. He hears it from the very moment that you are seized with helplessness, and He becomes actively engaged at once in hearing and answering the prayer of your helplessness.

O. Hallesby

I call on you, my God,
for you will answer me;
turn your ear to me and hear my prayer.

Psalm 17:6 (niv)

Every living thing needs a dwelling place—some place of safety to which it can retreat. Even the birds of the air that can quickly fly from anger need a refuge. A birdhouse provides them safety as our homes provide us with shelter. The church is also a place where we can escape from the storms of life. But God is our only true sanctuary. In Psalm 90:1(NIV), we read: *Lord, you have been our dwelling place throughout all generations.* And God is the sanctuary to which we can withdraw at any time because He dwells within us. He alone is our eternal Home.

The unthankful heart…
discovers no mercies;
but the thankful heart…
will find, in every hour,
some heavenly blessings.

HENRY WARD BEECHER

Give thanks to the LORD, *for he is good;*
his love endures forever.

PSALM 118:1 (NIV)

Have you ever read Hebrews 11, aka "The Faith Chapter," and marveled at the faith of the people listed there? It's like taking a walk through the Saints' Hall of Fame—Abel, Enoch, Noah, Abraham, Sarah, Isaac, Rahab, Jacob, Moses, and many more. They were all seemingly ordinary people who did amazing things for God. *I could never measure up*, you might think. But I have good news for you. Their hope is the *same* hope you have today. Their God is the *same* God you serve today. Their faith is the *same* faith you possess today. As a Christ follower, you are part of the larger tapestry of faith, weaving throughout history as part of God's plan. Someday that glorious plan will be complete, the picture will become crystal clear, and our faith will become sight.

JULIE CAMPBELL

I believe in the sun even if it isn't shining.
I believe in love even when I am alone.
I believe in God even when He is silent.

World War II Refugee

Faith is confidence in what we hope for and assurance about what we do not see.

Hebrews 11:1 (niv)

When incense burns, the smoke rises in a thin, wavering stream while it casts its thick fragrance all throughout the room. Imagine yourself as a small stick of incense that is constantly burning—the fragrance of your heart and mind always quietly streaming upward, revealing the thoughts, beliefs, and attitudes of who you really are. In Ephesians chapter 5, the apostle Paul says that if you live a life filled with love, following the example of Christ, you are sending up a sweet, pleasing aroma to God. But harboring bitterness and hatred in our hearts will produce a putrid stench. Will God smile when He "smells" the fragrance of your life today?

Mimi Klotz

Do all the good you can,
By all the means you can,
In all the ways you can,
In all the places you can,
At all the times you can.

Live a life filled with love,
following the example of Christ.
He loved us and offered himself
as a sacrifice for us,
a pleasing aroma to God.

Ephesians 5:2 (NLT)

When was the last time you held someone's hand? Were you keeping a child from danger? Strolling in the moonlight with someone dear? Making a business transaction? The grasp of a hand can mean many things and accomplish various purposes. When was the last time you "held" Jesus' hand? Were you desperate for healing? Or were you just enjoying time in His presence? Reach out for the Savior's hand, whatever your circumstances are. Psalm 138:7 (NIV) says, *You preserve my life...with your right hand you save me.* Let's place ourselves in the grip of our tender Creator today.

I long to accomplish a great
and noble task,
but it is my chief duty
to accomplish small tasks
as if they were great and noble.

HELEN KELLER

*I can do everything through Christ,
who gives me strength.*

PHILIPPIANS 4:13 (NLT)

To someone who has never set foot in the ocean, the water may seem a little intimidating. The tickle of the shoreline foam feels good on the toes, but it's another matter to trust yourself to the deep, perhaps cold unknown, of the water further out. We as Christians can experience the same uneasiness—God may seem a little intimidating at first, but as we learn to trust Him, we can wade deeper into His wonderful presence. Jesus said to Simon, *Put out into deep water, and let down the nets for a catch* (Luke 5:4 NIV). When we find the courage to wade deeper, we will discover similar treasure as we enjoy intimate fellowship with the Lord. Don't stay on the shore—wade deeper! Let God touch your heart. Enjoy the richness of all He has to offer you.

The best things are nearest: breath in your nostrils, light in your eyes, flowers at your feet, duties at your hand, the path of God just before you. Then do not grasp at the stars, but do life's plain common work as it comes, certain that daily duties and daily bread are the sweetest things in life.

ROBERT LOUIS STEVENSON

Every good and perfect gift is from above,
coming down from the Father
of the heavenly lights.

JAMES 1:17 (NIV)

Poised at the brink of something extraordinary—that's how each of us stands in relation to God. In many ways we are like the Apostle Peter, who from a storm-tossed ship, watched Jesus walk on water. Come, Jesus said. In the midst of our storm-tossed world, God calls us to trust Him. Perhaps by taking just one step, we may enter into God's plan—a plan that is different for each of us. Peter left us an important lesson—when he took his eyes off Jesus he began to sink. But when he cried out, *"Lord, save me!" Immediately Jesus reached out his hand and caught him* (Matthew 14:30–31 NIV). How reassuring! Even when we waver, we can call out to God—He'll hear and He'll help.

FLORA REIGADA

He touches our lives and leaves His imprint.
He encourages us and we are blessed.
He responds to us and we are transformed.
He hears our cries and brings us comfort.
In ever-deepening ways His love changes us…
and we are never the same.

Linda E. Knight

Direct my footsteps according to your word.

Psalm 119:133 (niv)

No matter the stress, no matter the pressures, no matter the struggles, God is here for you. Seek His strength and His wisdom. God can handle even the most difficult of circumstances, the most challenging of days. He is all-powerful, almighty, and all-loving. God will hear—and answer—your prayers.

Audrey Helbling

Each day is a gift wrapped in grace and wonder, a fresh chance to say "I love you," and to say, "Thank You, Jesus," for life and love and family. Each day is a new opportunity to pause long enough to celebrate the joy of just being alive. Each day is a gift awaiting your presence—unwrap the joy!

LINDA E. KNIGHT

This is the day the LORD has made.
We will rejoice and be glad in it.

PSALM 118:24 (NLT)

The journey of life takes us on many different roads. Some are straight, some winding, some smooth, some bumpy. You may not know what lies ahead, but rest assured—God knows and He promises never to leave you.

Karen Rhodes

Your word is a lamp for my feet,
a light on my path.

Psalm 119:105 (NIV)

Hope is a thousand stars to light
the darkened night,
a candle burning across eternity.
Hope is Jesus holding you so near,
you can hear His heartbeat.
Hope on!

Linda E. Knight

*Hope does not put us to shame,
because God's love has been poured out
into our hearts through the Holy Spirit.*

Romans 5:5 (NIV)

Not every road God chooses for us is sunlit and pleasant. In fact, some places seem shadowed and forbidding. These are the paths that test our faith. Can we find the strength to walk into the darkness, trusting God to guide and protect us? *Whoever dwells in the shelter of the Most High will rest in the shadow of the Almighty*, promises Psalm 91:1 (NIV). We may be surprised to find that the shadows we enter are actually underneath the wings of our Father, and the darkness is only the product of our own fears and weaknesses. Joy comes from walking into such a place, only to find that we have entered the presence of our Lord in an even deeper, more intimate way. We need not fear where the Lord may lead us. We can trust His loving care, even in the shadows.

Success is to be measured not so much by the position that one has reached in life as by the obstacles he has overcome trying to succeed.

Booker T. Washington

Commit your way to the Lord; trust in him and he will do this.

Psalm 37:5 (NIV)

How can we grasp the enormity of a limitless love? We look into the sky and see the tops of trees or gaze upon a mountaintop with wonder. We see the stars and try to fathom their distance and the vastness of the universe as a whole—it is wider, deeper, and higher than we can imagine. So is God's magnificent love! Are you discouraged? Have you lost someone you love? Do circumstances seem impossible? Do your sins seem beyond the scope of God's forgiveness? Remember, God's great love for you is more than a match for your most "hopeless" situation; His inexhaustible love covers absolutely every need.

The great thing in this world is
not so much where we are,
but in what direction we are moving.

Oliver Wendell Holmes

*Let us run with perseverance the race
marked out for us, fixing our eyes on Jesus,
the pioneer and perfecter of faith.*

Hebrews 12:1–2 (NIV)

How wonderful it is to think that Jesus journeys with us each day of our lives! When our way seems difficult, He goes before us to clear a path so that we may follow in His footsteps. We never have to fear that Jesus will lose the way because He has made the journey once before. He knows what it is like to be born and to live as a human being—even death holds no mystery for Him. And when we choose to ignore His guidance, Jesus doesn't abandon us to our own resources. He patiently waits for us to acknowledge that we cannot find the way on our own and welcomes us back with love and forgiveness. With thankful hearts, let's continue to follow Jesus and leave a trail of footprints for others seeking hope along the way.